MW01528922

SEEKING ENLIGHTENMENT
— WHY ?

Because 'enlightenment' means the end of
that load of suffering which stands between me and
the deep peace that I am seeking.

RAMESH S. BALSEKAR

Books by Ramesh S. Balsekar

- Pursue 'Happiness' And Get Enlightened (2008)
- Poniters From Ramana Maharshi (2008)
- Celebrate the Wit & Wisdom: Relax and Enjoy (2008)
- Koun Parva Karto?! [Marathi] (2008)
- Does The Human Being Have Free Will? (2007)
- Enlightened Living (2007)
- A Buddha's Babble (2006)
- A Personal Religion of Your Own (2006)
- The Essence of The Ashtavakra Gita (2006)
- The Relationship Between 'I' And 'Me' (2006)
- A Homage To The Unique Teaching of Ramesh S. Balsekar (2006)
- Nuggets of Wisdom (2005)
- The End of The Seeking (2005)
- Spiritual Search Step By Step (2004)
- Confusion No More (2003)
- Guru Pournima (2003)
- Upadesa Saram (2001)
- Advaita and The Buddha (2000)
- It So Happened That... (2000)
- Sin and Guilt: Monstrosity of Mind (2000)
- Meaningful Trivialities from the Source (2000)
- The Infamous Ego (1999)
- Who Cares?! (1999)
- The Essence of the Bhagavad Gita (1999)
- Your Head in the Tiger's Mouth (1997)
- Consciousness Writes (1996)
- Consciousness Strikes (1996)
- The Bhagavad Gita – A Selection (1995)
- Ripples (1994)
- Consciousness Speaks (1994)

SEEKING ENLIGHTENMENT — WHY ?

RAMESH S. BALSEKAR

EDITED BY
JAYA ARUN NAGARKATTI

ZEN
PUBLICATIONS

Copyright © 2005 By Ramesh S. Balsekar

First Edition: June 2005
Second Edition: December 2008

ISBN-10   81-88071-25-0
ISBN-13   978-81-88071-25-8

PUBLISHED BY

ZEN PUBLICATIONS

59, Juhu Supreme Shopping Centre, Gulmohar Cross Road No. 9,
JVPD Scheme, Juhu, Mumbai 400 049. India. Tel: +91 22 32408074
eMail: info@zenpublications.com Website: www.zenpublications.com

Credits: Cover & Book Design by Red Sky Designs, Mumbai

ACKNOWLEDGEMENT

The Publishers would like to thank Jyoti Gyanchandani for her invaluable help in
transcribing the conversation that appears on Page 89.

PRINTED BY

D. K. Printworld (P) Ltd., New Delhi

All rights reserved. No part of this book may be reproduced or transmitted by
any means, electronic or mechanical, including photocopying, recording, or by
any information storage and retrieval system without written permission from
the author or his agents, except for the inclusion of brief quotations in a review.

CONTENTS

All there is, is Consciousness.
Its movement is this Manifestation. Its movement
through a body is that body's life and destiny. There
truly is nothing else, unless Consciousness identifying
itself with a body: with its name and form as the Ego
considers itself the doer of its actions. That is the
beginning of the mechanism of *maya* – the original
sin. To know there is no 'doer' of any deed; that all
that happens is only a movement of God's energy or
Consciousness is the wisdom of all sages, no matter
what *prarabdhha*, or destiny each sage's
body has to undergo.

The Basic Problems of
the Spiritual Seeker

In the simplest, barest terms, the real problem of the
spiritual seeker is that, as a seeker, his very existence is
nothing but an apparent existence as sentience – nothing
more.

This is obviously because of the self-evident fact that
he himself as a 'fact' and 'self' does not exist at all. At
some point of time, the seeker is bound to realize, in his
innermost being, that it is a waste of time to seek any
satisfactory understanding of himself and his relation to
the surrounding universe through a self that simply cannot
be an autonomous individual.

The problem basically lies in the fact that it is this

7

essentially non-existing self which has to live his daily life! This is the real problem. The root of the problem lies in 'doership'. I have to do the daily living, and how can I do that living if 'I' do not exist?

This valid question, unfortunately, has been generally not given adequate attention. The attention has been centred on 'never forgetting that you are really the Source'. And this fact has made the confusion worse confounded:

'First, I really don't know who this is, who is doing the living; and then, additionally, I am told never to forget that I am the Source. If I concentrate on remembering I am the Source, who will concentrate on doing the living?'

There is a relatively simple solution to this maddening problem: The clear apperception of the seeker-self as the EGO. The *gravest error* in this respect has been that the self – the 'human being' – is supposed to have an ego; and the seeker-human being is expected to realize that the ego is the problem for his 'bondage' and that his 'freedom' depends on the annihilation of the ego. This error has been the cause of unimaginable confusion and frustration.

The really important point to understand, and remember, is that in phenomenal living, whether we think in terms of one human being or the entire humanity, the one concerned is always the ego, the separate entity – with total understanding, and therefore a 'sage'; or without the total understanding, and therefore an ordinary human being.

It is this ego, the separate entity, who has to do his daily living. The question, therefore, is: what does spiritual seeking mean to the ego?

The final spiritual understanding must clearly mean, after the awakened comprehension, comprehending one's total inexistence as an autonomous entity – i.e. *separate entities, yes; but not autonomous entities with volition.*

This clearly means that the seeker-entity is not the doer of any deed, and so long as the seeker-entity is doing anything 'himself' – or even deliberately not-doing it – no matter what he may be *doing*, and no matter how apparently unselfish and 'holy' it may be, nothing can ever be achieved.

The essence of the understanding is, in the words of the Buddha, 'events happen, deeds are done, consequences happen, but there is no individual doer of any deed.' This is because, in the absence of autonomy, the separate entity is, in *effect*, non-existent except as a psychosomatic apparatus. This comprehension, by suddenly snapping the phenomenally interminable chain of conceptualisation, would reveal the Noumenality whose immensity is the seeker-entity.

What this means, in simple practical terms, is the total comprehension that everything is a happening according to the Cosmic Law – no 'one' is doing anything and, therefore, no 'one' need be blamed for anything. In other words, there cannot be any autonomy for any separate entity, and, therefore, all separate entities are separate instruments through which the impersonal energy functions, and brings about whatever is to happen according to the Cosmic Law.

What do the Masters tell the ego-entity?
The Masters tell us that by understanding that what-we-appear-to-be is a fleeting shadow, a distorted and fragmentary reflection of what-we-all-are, we no longer

assume that we are this phenomenal appearance. It is a tragic fact that although this basic understanding is essentially simple and rather obvious, an enormous mass of structures – religious and philosophical – has been built around it in order to 'explain' it. As Wei Wu Wei says, 'In these psychic constructions men and women quite often spend their adult-lives elaborating devotional and sentimental, as well as intellectual personalities which hinder rather than help this ultimate understanding, which in itself is neither of a devotional, a sentimental, nor an intellectual character, but is very precisely the transcending of each, and the rejection of all three.'

But the real fact of the matter is that it is the seeker-entity who has to have this ultimate understanding, and, *at the same time*, to live his daily life. And this practical problem should never be underestimated, but unfortunately it is.

The individual seeker is told that he is in fact the Source
–'You are That' – but he has to live his life as a separate
entity, whatever his concept and conviction about his
'real nature'. This is the real difficulty which causes
enormous confusion and frustration, based inevitably on
the question: if I am the Source, surely I can do whatever
I like, *and*, the 'other', being the Source too, can do
whatever he likes. This would result in chaos. It would be
adding insult to injury in this situation for a Master to say
that 'all the anguish and despair they may experience is
inevitable, but it is beside the point.'

For me, therefore, there are two questions:

1. Do I tell the seeker that he is 'That', the Source, and let
him suffer the inevitable anguish and despair; or

2. Do I tell the seeker that it is the Source – Energy, Consciousness, God – which functions through all the body-mind organisms, all psychosomatic apparatuses; and the separate ego must live his life as a separate entity, with this conviction of the total inexistence of any autonomy and volition?

I definitely prefer the second alternative.

I would prefer to tell the seeker that, by 'himself', he can volitionally 'achieve' absolutely nothing, no matter what he may try to do or refrain from doing. This is because he would be working on an object, on a phenomenon, on a shadow in mind, instead of comprehending its own total inexistence as an *autonomous* entity. This comprehension by abruptly snapping the phenomenally interminable chain of conceptualisation – a sudden flash of acceptance that he simply cannot be the doer of any deed – would reveal the Noumenality whose immensity is all that he, and all entities, necessarily are.

The basic difficulty would still remain: If I am not the doer of any deed; how do I live my daily life?

Concerned with living one's daily life, another very relevant aspect of life has to be considered at this stage. What does the spiritual seeker ultimately want? Enlightenment – Self-realization – Being one with God – Knowing the Truth? But one has to go further: what does the seeker expect to get out of 'enlightenment' for the rest of his life that he did not have before? *This is truly the ultimate significance of the spiritual search.*
This has been the focus of my talks with visitors, during the last two years:

'What does the typical visitor – someone reasonably comfortable in life – want most, with the minimum understanding that no one has any control over the happening of life?'

The visitor who comes to me could be regarded as a spiritual seeker, and then the curious fact emerges that someone, reasonably comfortable in life, who is not a spiritual seeker would also be concerned with the same ultimate question in life: what would he want most in life?!

If we are looking for a direct, simple, short answer, it can only be: 'Happiness'.

So many people build their lives around pursuing pleasure, and end up in frustration, that we must clearly realize that the happiness one is seeking as the very basic necessity of one's life simply cannot be based on fleeting pleasures, for the simple reason that we have absolutely no control over the happening of life and 'life's slings and arrows'. Therefore, the happiness one is seeking as the most important thing in life must surely be something much deeper than pain or pleasure in the moment.

What all this comes to is a simple conclusion. We have absolutely no control over the happening of life from moment to moment. We cannot know whether the next moment will bring us pleasure or pain. Therefore the 'happiness' that one wants as the most important thing in one's life cannot depend on something over which one has no control. The final conclusion, therefore, is that our happiness in life cannot depend on the flow of life; *our happiness must necessarily depend on our attitude to life.* Our happiness cannot depend upon the vicissitudes of life; it must depend upon our attitude to life.

In order to consider our attitude to life, we must analyse our daily living and find out the basics of daily living. There are two essential basics to daily living:

1. Daily living means, basically, dealing with the situation in which one finds oneself: (a) to decide what one wants in a given situation, and (b) to do whatever one has to do in order to get what one wants. In other words, *'free will' is the basis of the mechanism of daily living.* But if we evaluate this 'free will' of the human being, both practically and theoretically, we cannot but come to the inevitable conclusion that our 'free will' is worth nothing; it is counterfeit.

Having once done whatever we wanted to do in a given situation, our free will ends, because what actually happens has never been in our control. What actually happens is one of three things: 1) we have got what we

wanted; 2) we have not got what we wanted; or
3) we have got what we never expected, for better or for
worse. We have never had any control over which of the
three alternatives happens. Therefore, the society takes
what has happened as our action, judges it as good or
bad, and gives us a reward or a punishment; the reward
means for us pleasure and the punishment means pain.
We have no choice but to accept it. And that is daily living
– sometimes pleasure, sometimes pain, on which our
happiness cannot depend. So, in practice, we have found
that our free will is worthless.

Now let us find out what our apparent free will means in
theory.

Our free will is based on two factors – one's genes and
one's conditioning; our conditioning includes whatever has
influenced our existing convictions about everything – our

SEEKING ENLIGHTENMENT—WHY?

education, our experience, our reading, our associations.

One had no control over being born to particular parents, and therefore, no control at all over our genes; and more and more research tells us that almost everything, physical or psychological characteristic, about any human being can be traced to some gene or the other. In other words, genes are such a powerful factor in one's personality. Similarly one had no control over being born to parents in a particular geographical environment or in a particular social background – upper class, upper-middle class, lower-middle class, or lower class – in which environment, both geographical and social, one received one's conditioning from day one. Conditioning at home, conditioning in social circle, conditioning in the school in that relevant environment, and conditioning in church or temple: this is right, that is wrong; this is sin and that is no sin; you must do this, you must not do that.

The result is that whatever one thinks or does depends on these two factors, over neither of which did one have the slightest control. When seen in this light, our apparent free will, even in theory, turns out to be not so genuine; in fact, counterfeit.

2. The second aspect of daily living means a relationship with the 'other' from morning till night. Dealing with a situation means dealing with the 'other', whether the other is a close relation like the wife or the son, or a neighbour or a business associate, or a total stranger. And the fact remains that I cannot be happy – at peace with myself, never uncomfortable with myself – if my relationship with the other is not harmonious. And here I come to a dead end – I cannot have happiness unless my relationship with the other is harmonious and I cannot expect every other

to be doing all the time what I expect him to do. Does it mean then that I cannot ever be authentically happy?

And yet, everyone knows at least one or two persons – even if they constitute a small number – who are transparently happy: they enjoy the same pleasures the others do, they suffer the same pains the others do, and are yet obviously happy – never uncomfortable with themselves, never uncomfortable with others.

So the focus of our enquiry becomes: what is the secret of the happy person? And the secret has been revealed to us, as far back as 2500 years, by the Buddha:

'Enlightenment means the end of suffering.'

What we have to find out for ourselves is: what is

this 'suffering' which prevents us from being 'happy'?
The suffering obviously is, as we have found out, our
relationship with the other – the basis of our daily living –
is not harmonious. The Buddha clearly tells us when this
suffering – the lack of a harmonious relationship with the
other – ends, the way is open for us to be happy.

And what is 'enlightenment' which ends the suffering?
Again the Buddha tells us with great clarity:
enlightenment means the *total* acceptance of the concept,
'Events happen, deeds are done, consequences happen, but
there is no individual doer of any deed.'

In other words, the Buddha tells us that everything is a
'happening' (according to the Cosmic Law), and how each
happening affects whom – for better or for worse – is
also according to the same Cosmic Law. The Cosmic Law
is obviously something so vast as to apply to the whole

universe for the entire infinity; and, therefore, totally beyond the comprehension of the feeble human intellect. Thus we cannot ever know the basis of the Cosmic Law; we can only accept every happening as something which had to happen according to the Cosmic Law.

The total acceptance of this concept of the Buddha means that no one can be blamed for any happening: neither oneself nor the other. Therefore, quite obviously, there can be no question of blaming the other for anything that happens through that body-mind organism. Therefore the relationship with the other must necessarily be always harmonious. And the fact that one does not blame oneself for anything means one does not have to carry any burden of guilt and shame for one's actions.

Who would not accept a lovely concept like this, which

frees one from the burden of guilt and shame for one's own actions and the burden of hatred for the other for his actions?

But the catch is that for the concept to actually work, the acceptance has to be not just intellectual but total.

At this stage, a valid difficulty arises: even if one is able to accept this concept totally, would it be possible for him to live his life, with this concept of personal non-doership, in a society which rejects this concept and holds everyone responsible for each action?

When this difficulty is presented to me, I have been able to say, quite confidently, that I have actually lived with this concept of personal non-doership for the last 20-odd years without the slightest difficulty.

My explanation is simple:
Daily living means in a given situation, I have decided
what I wanted and taken the necessary action; the
consequence has happened, and the society has taken
that consequence as my action. The society has judged
that action as 'good' or 'bad' and decided to 'reward'
me or 'punish' me – *I have no choice but to accept the
decision of the society, each time.* This has meant, in
practical living, pleasure (reward from society) or pain
(punishment from society), in the moment, from time to
time, from morning till night, from day to day.

And the point is that while I have accepted the
pleasure, the conviction that the action is not mine has
prevented any pride from arising in my ego; similarly,
the punishment resulting in 'pain' has not given rise
to any guilt in my ego. The result is that while I have
necessarily accepted the pleasure or pain awarded to

me by the society, my ego has remained pure, burdened with neither pride and arrogance nor guilt and shame. Therefore, peace of mind.

I would, therefore, say, from my own experience, that there is no practical difficulty in living life with the total acceptance that everything is a happening according to the Cosmic Law and that no one is to be blamed for any happening.

The other difficulty still remains to be tackled: how to make one's intellectual acceptance total acceptance. For this, I have a simple suggestion – what I call 'personal investigation.

Assuming you are busy throughout the day (otherwise you can do this exercise at any time) at the end of the day, take 20/30 minutes off, try to ensure that you will not be disturbed, and then be comfortable – this is not a hard discipline – and then do a very simple personal investigation:

From the many events during the day, most of which, you will agree, just happened without your volition, select one event which, you are sure, is your action.

And then investigate if it is your action: did I decide to do that action at any particular time?

Then you will recall that you did not and that, in fact what had happened was that you had had a thought and that thought had led to your action; if that thought had not happened, and you had had no control over its happening, what you now call your action would not have happened.

This personal investigation that you had done yourself must therefore push your intellectual acceptance of non-doership much deeper.

You may investigate any number of actions, and each time you will come to the conclusion, without exception, that it could not have been your action. And if you continue with this practice, at some point of time, depending on the Cosmic Law and your destiny, it is more than likely that a *flash* of total acceptance will happen: I simply cannot be the doer of any action, and what is more, the 'other' cannot be the doer of any action either, whether or not he or she knows it. And then, no doubts can remain.

The total acceptance of non-doership provides a special bonus for the seeker a) no mistake and b) no sin. So my free will is based on two factors over which I have no control. My free will is based on two factors

29

– genes and conditioning which God made. I repeat, if whatever I have just done is because of two factors which God made, isn't it perfectly clear, that whatever I have just done, good, bad or indifferent – whatever the consequences – whatever I have just done is exactly what God wanted me to do. I repeat: if whatever I just have just done is based on two factors which God made – is it not perfectly clear, whatever I have just done and whatever the consequences, I have done precisely what God wanted me to do?! So, if I have just done precisely what God wanted me to do, how can I make a mistake? Whatever the consequences, having done precisely what God wanted me to do, 'I' cannot make a mistake! Therefore, with this understanding, for the last 20 odd years I have not wasted any time or energy in trying to locate 'my' mistake, nor any thought on how to avoid that in future. Everybody knows...we are wasting an enormous amount of time and energy in asking: where

have I gone wrong? I didn't succeed, where did I go
wrong? What mistake did I commit?...Now I don't waste
my time on anything like this! I cannot make a mistake!

And for many, many many people the more important
point is, having done exactly what God wanted me to do,
how can I commit a sin? How can I ever commit a sin?

Therefore at any moment I have just done what I wanted
to do, and yet, my logical analysis tells me, I cannot
commit a sin. And if I cannot commit a sin I don't have
to be afraid of any God who might want to punish me.
And if I don't have to fear God, nothing prevents me from
loving God...as my Creator.

In the absence of personal doership – volition – what is the
human being?

It is interesting to note that the world-famous American humorist had left a piece of writing which he subsequently published privately as a book *What is Man?* – a book that is obviously not very well known. It was an essay in popular philosophy, written in a style of extreme simplicity and patently aimed at the average reader. The core of the book is built around a few definitive ideas which Mark Twain announced as 'final truths of experience'.

In the preface to the semi-private edition, he said, 'every thought in these pages has been thought, and accepted as unanswerable truth, by millions upon millions of men – and concealed, kept private. Why did they not speak out? Because they dreaded (and could not bear) the disgust of the people around them.'

Mark Twain must have been under a compelling sense

that America needed to have the points made in the book proclaimed aloud and driven home.

The principles – perhaps dogmas – stated in precise terms, are four in number:

(1) Man is a machine; he originates nothing, not even a thought. He is moved, directed, commanded, by external influences alone.

(2) All conduct arises from a single motive – self-satisfaction; the attainment of self-approval. Man must act so as to content the spirit within; he cannot do otherwise.

(3) The permanent unalterable thing in a human being is the temperament. Born with a man, the temperament remains with him to the end; he cannot change it.

(4) Complete determinism. Man is made by his heredity;

the future, being fixed, is as irreversible as the past. In *What is Man?* Mark Twain makes the following remarks

1. What is the sole impulse that ever moves a person to do a thing? The impulse to *content his own spirit* – the *necessity* of contenting his own spirit and *winning its approval*. The unselfish man may think he is doing something solely for the other person's sake, but it is not so; he is contenting – his own spirit first – the other person's benefit has to always take *second* place.

2. What about the lofty and gracious passion of mother-love? It is the absolute slave of the law. The mother will go naked to clothe her child; she will starve that it may have food; suffer torture to save it from pain; die that it may live. She takes a living *pleasure* in making these sacrifices. She does it for that reward, that self-approval,

that contentment, that peace, that comfort.

3. What about duty for duty's sake? *It does not exist.* Duties are not performed for duty's sake, but because their *neglect* would make the man *uncomfortable.*

4. We (mankind) have ticketed ourselves with a number of qualities to which we have given misleading names. Love, Hate, Charity, Compassion, Avarice, Benevolence, and so on. We attach misleading *meanings* to the names. They are all forms of self-contentment, self-gratification, but the names so disguise them that they distract our attention from the fact. Also, we have smuggled a word into the dictionary which ought not to be there at all – self-sacrifice. It describes a thing which does not exist. There is only one sole Impulse which dictates and compels a man's every act: the imperious necessity of securing his own approval, in every emergency and at all costs.

5. There are none but temporary Truth-seekers – a permanent one is a human impossibility; as soon as the seeker finds what he is thoroughly convinced as the truth, he seeks no further, but gives the rest of his days to hunting junk to patch it and caulk it and prop it with, and make it weather-proof and keep it from caving in on him. Hence the Presbyterian remains a Presbyterian, the Mohammedan a Mohammedan, the Spiritualist a Spiritualist, the Democrat a Democrat, the Republican a Republican, the Monarchist a Monarchist – for Man is nothing but an automatic machine and must obey the law of his construction.

[Pope John Paul II announced in India: The final salvation can only be through Jesus Christ].

6. Granting that dumb animals are able to think upon a low plane, is there any that can think upon a high one?

Is there one that is well up towards man? Yes. As a thinker and planner the ant is the equal of any savage race of man; as a self-educated specialist in several arts she is the superior of any savage race of man; and in one or two high mental qualities she is above the search of any man, savage or civilized.

In all his history the aboriginal Australian never thought out a house for himself and built it. The ant is an amazing architect. She is a wee little creature, but she builds a strong and enduring house eight feet high – a home which is as large in proportion to her size as is the largest capitol or cathedral in the world compared to man's size. No civilized race has produced architects who could plan a home better for the uses proposed than can hers. Her house contains a throne-room; nurseries for her young; granaries; apartments for her soldiers, her workers, etc.; and they and the multifarious halls and corridors which communicate with them are arranged and distributed with an educated and experienced eye for convenience and adaptability. The ant discriminates between friend and stranger. Sir John Lubbock took ants from three different nests, made them drunk with whiskey, and laid them, unconscious, by one of the nests, near some water. Ants from three nests came and examined and discussed these disgraced creatures, then carried their friends home and threw the strangers overboard! Sir John repeated the experience a number of times – for a time the sober ants did as they had done at first. But finally they lost patience, and threw both friends and strangers overboard!

7. Beliefs are *acquirements*, temperaments are *born; beliefs are subject to change, nothing whatever can change temperament.*

[Temperaments are dictated by the genes, beliefs are

conditioning].

The essential understanding is simple enough: what we are is not the phenomenal appearance but *That* which functions through this appearance. Intellectually, some degree of this understanding is neither uncommon nor difficult to acquire, but only a small fraction of those who have this intellectual understanding ever reach the totality of the understanding itself – when the 'I understand' disappears. They will often work hard, following techniques and methods, religious or otherwise; they will even devote their whole lives to it.

But all this is to no purpose as long as they cling to the illusion that they themselves are individual entities putting in great effort to acquire something. They may succeed in comprehending the emptiness, the voidness of objective things, in fulfilling all the conditions laid down by the

Masters and their *ashrams* and schools, but the point is that as long as they 'themselves' are doing it – and perhaps cannot help feeling a certain amount of pride in their achievement – no matter what they may be doing, or deliberately not doing, and no matter how apparently altruistic and 'holy' it may be, the apperception cannot happen until and unless they comprehend their own total inexistence as *autonomous* entities. In Huang Po's phrase, they are using mind to find mind, and mind cannot find mind any more than an eye can see itself.

The final understanding has repeatedly been described as 'sudden', 'a flash', or 'immediate' for the simple reason that it is the realization of intemporality. It can only be 'sudden' that is timeless, because our psyche is incapable of registering it; that is why it cannot be a psychosomatic 'experience', though, of course, a phenomenon – a body-mind instrument – has to be the medium or vehicle for that happening. Once more – and it cannot be reflected too often – no amount of 'self-improvement', self-cultivation', 'self-negating', through whatever method, can ever achieve the final understanding so long as it is being 'done' by an entity. The reason is simple – it can only be a sudden happening, from the superior dimension of intemporality.

It is this very fact which causes the basic problem in the spiritual search.

Anyone reasonably well qualified can write a book about any aspect of human knowledge and maintain that it states the truth in so far as it is known at the time of writing. This can be done because it is the objective understanding that is concerned. But when the spiritual search is concerned, it cannot be taught methodically. All that a Master, a sage, a man of understanding can do is to manoeuvre the seeker into turning around in the right direction, that he might one day apprehend the truth for himself, *subjectively*. What words can do is to enable the reader to start the journey during which the truth that can never be written, or described vocally, is approached gradually by 'intuition rendered dualistically'. Indeed, to try to understand the Truth at the hands of others is to close the gates of Self-realization. The main problem is that words can be misunderstood and misused.

For instance,

1. Take the word 'meditation'. We know what the normal man meant by it: 'meditation is discursive, rambling mental activity by means of images, forms and figures that are produced imaginatively'. And yet most Masters agree that that is the first thing to be

got rid of. The great sage Ashtavakra is directly more emphatic. He says *doing* meditation is the great obstacle to the happening of the ultimate understanding. Yet, presumably because it is one of the meanings found in a Sanskrit dictionary for the word *Dhyana*, we are faced with that 'method' of 'attaining' enlightenment. The accepted meaning of the word among the Masters is, of course, 'awareness', implying a vivid state of consciousness free of all meditation of any kind. There are various other substitutes like 'contemplation' and 'concentration' which are equally unhappy. Perhaps a more useful would be, simply, 'non-objective awareness'.

2. 'Self-sacrifice'

Deliberate 'altruism' really has no spiritual value because it is based on the subject-object relationship of phenomenal living, and therefore 'egoism'. We think of the sage serving others, and we feel we should imitate him. But does the sage really think whatever he does is for 'others'? Not really. Whatever the sage seems to be doing is, in his own eyes, something that is happening, and not his own 'doing'.

3. 'Love'

Is there really any such thing as 'love' in reality? What we seek to describe by that word is emotion experienced in certain highly personal channels charged with possessiveness, shadowed by jealousy, with its counterpart 'hate' ever ready to take its place. So a sage does not love or hate; he only knows pure affectivity which does not pace through egoistic channels and therefore cannot be interpreted at all. The sage's affectivity, in its pure state, is what may be known as *Karuna*: Love without its opposite Hate, in the absence

SEEKING ENLIGHTENMENT-WHY?

of the subject-object relationship.

Finally let me remind you:

1. The beingness of separate entities is non-separate being.

2. Being present with absence of being a separate entity is absolute absence.

3. Stepping into the public hall, Huang Po, the Master said:

> 'The knowledge of many things cannot be compared for excellence with giving up seeking for anything. There are not different kinds of mind, and there is no doctrine which can be put into words.
>
> 'As there is no more to be said, the assembly is dismissed.'

4. The transcendence of pleasure-and-pain can be attained not by wallowing in either, but by *experiencing* the transitoriness of either.

5. Is it not an obvious fact of life that what is perceived – an object – cannot possibly perceive?!

Finally let me assure you that all I can do for you readers, or for those who take the trouble to visit me, is to turn you around, and set you facing in the right direction, and place you with your backs to the phenomenal object, by offering you my concepts. I have no truth to pass on to you.

The Spiritual Circuitry of the Brain

Andrew Newberg M.D. has brought out a book on the brain science behind religious and mystical experience: *Why God Won't Go Away.*

'Something happens in your brain when you forgive someone or express love and gratitude,' says Newberg. 'Humility and altruism all have a philosophical basis, an emotional basis, and a neurological basis. We are just starting to develop techniques to look at these things. The scans have opened a window to a huge variety of experiences and ways of thinking.'

Louise Danielle Palmer, the deputy editor of *Spirituality & Health* magazine, says further on this subject, that something like forgiveness requires a sense of self and of the rest of the world which comes mainly from the brain's frontal and parietal lobes. The same would, of course, apply to humility and tolerance of the other, based on the fact that everything is a happening according to the Cosmic Law and not the deed done by any individual entity.

It also involves, says Palmer, an emotional memory, which is tied to the hippocampus and the temporal lobes, to recognize when someone has hurt us. Forgiveness also involves a cognitive process of changing our minds, to see a person or problem in a different light. Acceptance of the fact that what has hurt us is a happening and not the body-mind organism – the psychosomatic apparatus – through which the happening has happened, means seeing the event in a totally different light.

Depending on one's nature, this might happen in the

SEEKING ENLIGHTENMENT-WHY?

limbic system, which is responsible for emotion, if one relies on reason, not blaming anyone or forgiving someone could involve the temporal lobe, the site of analytic and mathematical abilities. If one has a holistic bent, it could involve the right parietal lobe that creates the feeling of connection. How you decide not to blame anyone – or forgive someone – depends on how you access the 'system' to re-establish a sense of fresh relationship and create a good feeling, which is relayed to the region that controls behaviour.

Says Newberg: 'This has tremendous implications for clinical research and psychotherapy. It's not about saying stop the Prozac, which might be necessary for some, but rather saying that therapy might include spiritual practices.

'This is what psychotherapy is all about; it's what going

to church is all about: how to modify your thoughts [thinking] and behaviour to feel better and have more success in your relationships. It might help people understand the different ways they are capable of forgiving...If we can figure out what's going on when people stop forgiving or stop loving, may be we can help them.'

This might seem like soft and fuzzy stuff but let us not forget that this comes from a hard-core specialist in nuclear medicine. But it so happens that Newberg is a 'spiritual guy' who just happens to have a big brain, a spiritual seeker who, when a little kid, had questions so pressing that that they would wake him in the middle of the night, get him out of bed, and lead him into his father's den: How do we know Cod exists? Why is there good and evil? How would I know what is real?

Andrew Newberg's exploration of neurotheology is based on a decade of intellectual partnership with Eugene D'Aquili, M.D., a psychiatrist at the University of Pennsylvania, whom Newberg describes as 'the most brilliant man I have ever met.' Within the first year of their collaboration, they had developed a theoretical model for something never before illustrated: *the spiritual circuitiy of the brain.*

By building a bridge between science and spirituality, Newberg believes we can achieve what many doctors, physicists and theologians consider impossible: to pinpoint the origin of consciousness.

Newberg and D'Aquili were instrumental in creating the machine SPECT (Single Photon Emission Computed Tomography) which enabled them to test their theoretical model and capture the now-famous snapshot of the brain in the moment of spiritual transcendence, a state variously known in its highest form as *samadhi, nirvana,* God-consciousness, or 'Absolute Unitary Being', a term they coined.

Newberg and D'Aquili began their study with a group of devout practitioners of Tibetan Buddhist meditation. The images Newberg captured on the SPECT machine showed that 'the brain's pre-frontal cortex, called the seat of attention, lit up in a brilliant vermillion, indicating an increase in blood flow, or neural activity, due to the meditator's state of deep concentration. However, the upper rear area of the brain, known as the orientation association area, had gone dark. This is where we get our ability to orient ourselves in space and time, which gives our bodies a sense of physical limits. It is also where the brain 'makes' sense of our individual self existing in – and apart from – the physical universe.'

The darkness in the upper rear area of the brain told Newberg that 'when a meditator took a metaphysical dive inside, the outside world receded, effectively blocking the sensory input that ordinarily streams into our brains.' As a result, the brain has no choice but to perceive that 'self' as endless, interconnected with everything and everyone.

The results also revealed something astonishing: 'The thalamus was asymmetrical suggesting that the brain structure of serious spiritual practitioners differs from most people's. Whether their brains are different as a result of spiritual practice, or whether they were attracted to the practice because their brains were different to begin with, is still an open question.'

The question is: are the brain scans giving us a glimpse of that place Newberg calls Absolute Unitary Being (AUB) that mystics have claimed as being far more 'real' than our daily 'reality'? 'Informed speculation tells us that AUB is a reality from which all objective and subjective perspectives are derived,' Newberg writes in *Why God Wont Go Away*. 'Whether or not it is real, it provides us with a common source of all spiritual urges and a universal goal that has been interpreted in myriad ways by all the great religions of the past and present.'

The brain scans show that our brains are expert at bringing consciousness in and at coalescing it into an individual entity, but the fact remains that the brain is not responsible for consciousness, as such. It is merely a vehicle by which consciousness can be manifested. The point is that consciousness or pure awareness is the fundamental 'stuff' of the universe, and that consciousness is what abounds everywhere. Of course it is also a fact we cannot know how our physical world came out of consciousness. We cannot get out of our brains to know what is actually out there – if anything at all – for the simple reasons that 'we' are trapped in our own consciousness.

It is a fact of life that when we focus on one source of sensory input – whether it is a sound or an image – we deprive the brain of other kinds of information. Focus and contemplation make us more likely to feel 'one with everything'. But the fact remains that it can only lead to a time-bound experience. For that experience to become a part of our very being, what is needed is a basic total acceptance of the Buddha's basic principle – a total in mind *and heart* – that everything is a happening according to the Cosmic Law for which no individual entity can be blamed, neither oneself nor the other. In other words, every single apparent, separate entity is only an instrument through which the One Source, by whatever label we understand It, functions, and brings about whatever is supposed to happen at that time and place, according to the Cosmic Law. This brings about a harmonious relationship with the 'other' and peace of mind for oneself – the peace of mind which keeps us 'one with everything' all the time.

What the scans have clearly shown is that the human longing to connect with something larger than ourselves is grounded in our biology and manifested in the very wiring of the brain. Whatever sceptics may say, mystical religious states can no longer be written off as the result of wishful thinking or emotional confusion. The ultimate fact of the matter, however, is that the final understanding must happen not in the brain but in the heart, not an intellectual acceptance but a total acceptance. The acceptance has to be total that the individual separate entity is indeed the separate entity that has to live his or her life in the circumstances in which he or she has been placed by the Source or Consciousness, but that this entity has no autonomy or volition but is merely an instrument through which the Source or Consciousness functions and brings about whatever is supposed to happen according to the Cosmic Law; and that, therefore, no one is to be blamed for any happening – neither oneself nor the other.

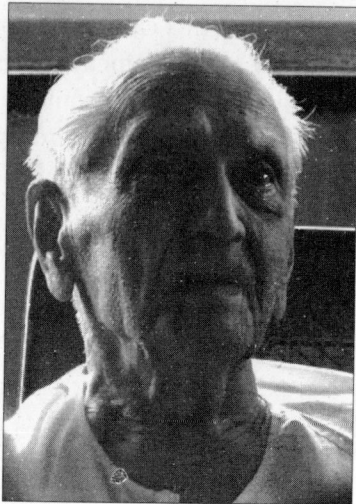

The Ultimate Insight

Knowing what can there be nothing more
to be known? That there never has been
any objective 'being', that no objective
appearance can ever have the beingness of the
One Source; and that, therefore, no object
can ever be the Subject — doer of
any deed.

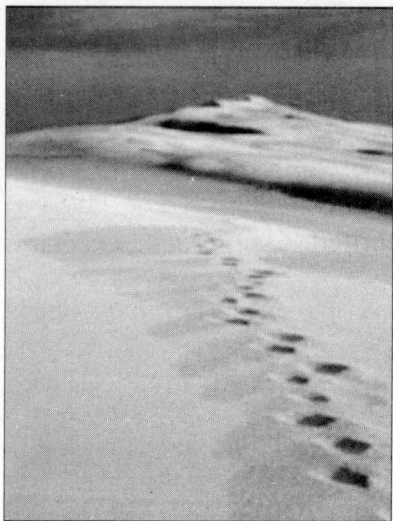

Spiritual Search
...Step by Step

1 The basic concept is that every event, big or small, must happen according to God's Will / Cosmic Law. It is impossible for the human being to understand the basis of this Law because he has not been given the intellect powerful enough to ever comprehend it. It is too vast and too complex.

2 The very start of the spiritual search begins only because it is supposed to happen according to a Cosmic Law. All further effort depends on the destiny of the individual concerned. Any worrying about the spiritual 'progress' is unnecessary, frustrating and indeed itself an obstacle.

3 The actual circumstances in which the search begins can vary vastly depending on the individual concerned. It can be an inherent part of the genes so that, even as a child, there are questions he asks which do not interest others, and which parents and teachers are unable to answer. Or perhaps, because of a particular event, such as a bereavement in the family. Finally, it could occur quite late in life with the arising of a question: I have everything anyone wants – money, fame, good health – and though I have certainly been enjoying life, why is it that I have this nagging feeling of being incomplete, unfulfilled?

4 Once the seeking starts, how it progresses, and where it will end depends entirely on the individual's destiny according to the Cosmic Law. The most important point is that 'enlightenment' is not something to be achieved, but it is a happening through an entity, as a part of

the totality of life. The body-mind organism is only an instrument through which the event occurs. Considerable confusion and frustration can arise if this fact is not taken into consideration. And, of course, even this would be destined!

5 Is a guru necessary? The answer is simple: if according to the Cosmic Law, the guru is needed, you and your guru will be brought together by circumstances. You do not have to worry about it.

6 What path do I follow? The path will be revealed precisely when it is supposed to according to the Cosmic Law.

7 What is the seeking all about? The usual answer is 'enlightenment'. The core of the matter, however, is one

63

that is not, unfortunately, usually addressed. The answer should not end merely with a concept like enlightenment. The seeker must ask: what do I expect the event of enlightenment to do for me, the seeker, for the rest of my life that I did not have before? The essential fact is that the seeker, as a separate entity, must live the rest of his life in more or less the same circumstances, even after the search ends successfully. This not being kept in mind, considerable angst arises.

8 The seeker must ask this question to the guru, teacher or mentor: 'What can I expect from enlightenment, and how will it enhance the rest of my life?' The genuine guru will give you a straightforward answer. Otherwise, you can expect an answer like, 'When enlightenment happens, there will be no more you to ask this question.' This is not really true. The

sage, even after full and total understanding, has to
live the rest of his life as the same entity in similar
circumstances. What then is the differene in his life?

9 The answer to this question has been given in the
most succinct manner by the Buddha: 'Enlightenment
means the end of suffering.' What could the Buddha have
meant by the word 'suffering'? Obviously, not the pain
in the moment which every sage has suffered even after
enlightenment. The suffering which the Buddha referred
to is that which the seeker has created for himself by
believing that each action is done by a separate entity, and
not accepting that every event is a happening according to
the Cosmic Law.

10 The suffering is the enormous load of guilt and
shame for his own actions, together with the even heavier
load of hatred and malice towards the other for actions

that caused 'me' hurt. It is this burden that disappears instantly as one is able to accept *totally* that everything is a happening according to a Cosmic Law, including all actions which have apparently occurred through the various body-mind organisms.

11 At this juncture, questions could arise: 'What about one's responsibility to society?' 'Would this concept of non-doership, appealing though it is, not encourage the ordinary individual to go on a rampage, committing crimes that he would otherwise hesitate to do?' This argument would not hold good for two reasons. Firstly, the ordinary individual's programming – genes plus conditioning – would simply not allow him to indulge in a crime merely because according to a particular concept he is not the doer of any action. Only the psychopath could do this, since he is

programmed to do so. Secondly no one can ever abandon his responsibility to the society in which he lives whatever his personal conviction. The society would still hold him accountable for his misdemeanors and punish him accordingly.

12 A further query could be: 'Even assuming I am able to accept this concept totally, would it be possible for anyone to actually live his life according to this principle of non-doership in a society that does not subscribe to it and holds everyone responsible for their actions?' Here I can verify that not only is it possible, but quite easy to do so. I have lived my life for the last 20 years with an extraordinary amount of simplicity, abiding by this concept: Living my life actually means nothing more than doing whatever I have to do at any time in a given situation. Suppose in a given situation I have done

whatever I thought I should do – which is all any one is expected to do. Thereafter, the matter is out of my hands and I have to accept whatever the society decides about 'my' action, according to the social regulations and legal provisions. On a particular occasion, the society may decide that my action was a really good one and has benefited a lot of people. And I therefore should be rewarded. This verdict of the society brings pleasure in the body-mind organism, which I would thoroughly enjoy in the moment. But, *knowing* that it was really not my action, but a happening through my body-mind organism, there simply cannot arise the slightest pride or arrogance in my ego. Then, to go to the other extreme, if the society condemns an action as a bad action, that has hurt several people, this verdict would certainly bring about a feeling of pain and regret in the body-mind organism. But, *knowing* that it was not really my action, the pain or regret would not be accompanied by any feeling of guilt or shame in the ego. Life means living from moment to moment, doing whatever one has to do in any situation. When I accept the verdict of society, from time to time, pain or pleasure will continue to arise in the body-mind organism in the moment, but my ego will be totally free of both guilt and shame, and pride and arrogance. For the last 20 years, 'life' has meant for me pleasure or pain according to my destiny, but my ego has always been free of the additional burden.

13 Accepting that it is possible for me to live my life in society with my concept of non-doership, what about the hurt that I might receive from the other while living my life? Prior to having the total acceptance of non-doership, whenever I was hurt my reaction was: 'He has hurt me and I hate him.' Now with the understanding that it

is a happening which has hurt me because it was my destiny, through whom it occurred is quite irrelevant. Therefore, it would be stupid to hate an instrument. There is no question of hating anyone for what happens. The net result is that daily living has meant momentary pleasure or pain, according to my destiny, through events which may happen through any body-mind organism – mine or the other's – which I have to accept. But my ego has remained pure, untainted by any trace of pride or arrogance, guilt or shame, jealousy or envy, hatred or malice.

14 I have thus lived for 20 years like any other citizen, in a society which holds me responsible for 'my' actions. I have come across no practical difficulty in living with my concept that everything is a happening according to a Cosmic Law, and that each individual

has to live as a separate entity. The only difference in my thinking – now and before – is that now I am totally convinced that each separate entity, necessarily living his life, is in actuality an instrument through which life flows as a series of happenings.

15 Since the understanding and acceptance of nondoership has to be total, and not just intellectual, a vitally important question remains: 'What does one do to make it total?' In otherwords, '*What do I have to do to be able to accept totally that I am not the doer?!*' The obvious answer is: 'Nothing!' It will *happen* only if it is supposed to happen, according to one's destiny as per the Cosmic Law.

16 The seeker's question now takes another shape: 'While I am waiting for something to happen, is

there not something I can do as a spiritual practice, assuming that doership is still there?' I do have a suggestion for such a spiritual practice, which I call 'Self Investigation'. It is not a difficult discipline, but a simple investigation. At the end of the day, assuming you are busy throughout the day, take 20-30 minutes off, and sit quietly but comfortably. Since this is not a discipline, you are welcome to sip on a cup of coffee, a glass of beer or whatever you may like. Then do some very simple investigation:

From the many events of the day, some of which you will accept are not your actions, select one which you are convinced is your action. Of others you are not so sure, but this one you are certain of and are willing to take any bet on it. Then investigate: 'If it is my action, did I decide to do it at a particular time?' The answer every time would be: 'No, I did not.' Then how did the action happen? You realize that it occurred because you had a thought which led to it. If that thought had not arisen – over which you had no control – 'your' action would not have taken place. Therefore, you cannot really call it your action. This investigation, resulting in your conviction – that the action you thought was yours turned out not to be so – makes your acceptance of non- doership go deeper every time you conduct an investigation. Now, take up another action that you think is yours. And then another. And every time, without exception. you will come to the conclusion that what you thought was your action depended upon the happening of another event over which you had no control. If you had not happened to be at a particular place at a particular time and seen, heard, smelt, tasted or touched something – what you called your action would not have happened. You cannot therefore call that action yours. If you are able to continue this practice regularly, it is more than likely that at a certain point of time, depending on your destiny according to the Cosmic Law, a flash of total acceptance will happen: *'I simply cannot be the doer.'* And when that flash happens, there will no longer be any doubts or questions. Then the acceptance has become total.

The corollary of this understanding, of course, is that no one else either can be the doer of their actions, whether *they* know it or not.

17 To recapitulate, the basic concept is that everything is a happening, and not anyone's doing. Therefore, in the case of spiritual seeking, there is really no seeker doing any seeking but seeking happening

through a particular body-mind organism as a separate
entity. Indeed, this is not limited only to spiritual seeking.
For a particular kind of seeking to happen, be it for
wealth, fame or power, it happens according to a Cosmic
Law. The body-mind organism concerned is appropriately
programmed through the genes, and conditioning
received at home, in society, school, church or temple.
The seeking begins as a natural happening, but when
the ego is created, the doer comes into being as the
individual seeker, thinking he is in charge of the seeking.
It is only the spiritual seeker who, if he is destined to
have the final, ultimate understanding, realizes the
absurdity of personal doership – and enlightenment
happens through a particular body-mind organism. No
one is enlightened. It must be borne in mind that this
happening need not happen in one lifetime. The process
could well take several lifetimes. 'Whose lifetimes?'
would be a futile question. Each lifetime has a particular

body-mind organism and a particular ego attached to that organism for the duration of that specific lifetime. At what stage of development the spiritual seeking starts in a particular lifetime of an entity is something determined entirely according to the Cosmic Law. Thus in the body-mind organism called *Ramana Maharishi*, the process was almost complete through previous lives, and the full enlightenment happened in him, without any personal effort at all, at the very early age of 16 years.

18 To conclude, no one becomes enlightened, no one achieves enlightenment. Enlightenment happens through a particular body-mind organism, according to the Cosmic Law, as a part of life and living.

The fundamental understanding is that the ONE

unmanifest source has become the many in the manifold universe. The functioning of the manifestation – 'life' as we know it – is based on the duality of interconnected opposites of every conceivable kind, beginning with male and female. The Source is the Unicity, unmanifest, which has become the two in the manifested appearance; so duality is the basis of the manifestation, and its functioning that we know as life. The sage has been able to accept the basic duality of life; the ordinary person, not being able to accept it, lives in *dualism,* constantly choosing one opposite against the other and lives in frustration.

Formula for Daily Living

Humility within and tolerance for the other, contentment within and compassion for the other, not as something to be pursued, but as something that aries as a natural result of the understanding that everything is a happening according to the Cosmic Law for which no one is to blame, neither oneself nor the other.

The Sage
A Man of Wisdom

1 THE SAGE, a man of wisdom, is a symbol of that mysterious virtue and supernal simplicity; a messenger of peace and harmony, a herald of humility.

2 HIS OWN daily living is striking testimony of the practicality of his basic concepts that might seem at first sight to be idealistic but impractical.

3 HIS DAILY talks take place regularly with such apparent ease and flow, and there is no one to claim any merit.

4 THE SAGE never magnifies himself; thus he becomes perfect in his greatness. He seems to do all things

silently, mysteriously, effectively.

5 HIS TEACHING – his 'set of concepts' – is so marvellous in its immaculate simplicity that those who find it and delight in it, often times do not know it because they are like little children. While those who seek it, do not find it because their minds are not vacant like those of little children, but full of proud learning.

6 IN THE SAGE'S daily living there is much to suggest the ebb and flow, the action and interaction, of existence and non-existence, of the higher and the lower, of the inner and the outer, of the strong and the weak, of the positive and the negative, of the full and the empty, of the expansion and the contraction – all this with great felicity, as there is no implication of dualism. There is the total acceptance of the underlying

unity between the unmanifest and the manifest, between the deep understanding and the daily living.

7 THE SAGE accomplishes a great deal, but does not identify himself with the deed nor with its merit, but retires into himself and abides in peace and serenity.

8 THE SAGE is never unaware that the soft and the hard, the strong and the weak, and all such opposites, are the essential elements of the duality of manifestation and its functioning that we know as 'life'. Therefore, the sage recognizes his utter dependence on the Divine, and his strength is perfected in weakness. The sage is fully aware – but not conscious – that he has several 'faults' along with his good points. Hence the humility.

9 THE SAGE does not lay up treasure: his riches are within. The more he gives to others, the more he has of

his own. He is considerate of the ideas of others, never forgetting the essential unities. He lives in the world, yet remains withdrawn. He lives in accord with mankind, yet remains himself.

10 THE SAGE has three treasures to which he holds fast: compassion, economy and humility. Through compassion he shows courage; through economy he can give freely to others; through humility he becomes a 'vessel of the highest honour'.

11 THE SAGE, being fully aware that 'love' and 'hate' are both based on what the other has done, and therefore really do not exist, lives his daily life accepting whatever each happening brings in the moment – sometimes pain, sometimes pleasure – as something supposed to happen according to the Cosmic Law. His relationship with the other is therefore always

harmonious, and this leads to his own constant peace of mind.

12 MIND'S ESSENTIAL peace is disturbed when the deeper meaning of life is not understood. Everything is a happening according to the Cosmic Law, which is concerned with the entire universe for all eternity. There is no action done by any individual entity. When this is understood, there is peace and harmony. The sage does not try to achieve passivity by stopping activity, having realized that the very effort itself generates activity.

13 THE MIND of the sage exists undisturbed in the Way of the Cosmic Law, without any trace of 'this or that', 'right or wrong'. The mind-essence is never lost in confusion. Nothing is taken personally. And thus nothing can offend any longer. Peace and harmony prevails.

14 IT IS DISTINCTLY noticeable that the sage, in his daily living, seems to do his routine work not only effortlessly but extremely efficiently. This is really not difficult to understand. The 'thinking mind' of the sage being absent, the 'working mind' of the sage is not hampered by illusory fears creating unnecessary problems in an illusory future. When the thinking-objects vanish, the thinking-subject also vanishes.

15 AFTER THE ultimate understanding has happened, the sage suddenly realizes, with a certain amount of surprise, that to have been attached to the idea of enlightenment was the obstacle. Enlightenment is not an achievement, not an end in itself. It is a happening which brings peace and harmony to the entity concerned, who continues to face the rest of his life from moment to moment.

16 THE SAGE realizes how astonishingly simple and innocent is that which at one time seemed such an insurmountable impasse: the problem of bondage, freedom and enlightenment. It is so obvious. Each separate entity obeys its own nature conferred upon it by God: over this, it has no choice. It is impossible for any puny human brain to understand God's Will. Where is the question of right and wrong? Every happening will have its own consequence, be it happiness or unhappiness. It is the burdensome practice of judging that brings weariness, and prevents the acceptance of 'what-is' in the moment.

17 THE SAGE has understood that enlightenment does not mean escaping from the world of sense and ideas, but participating in it totally with peace and equanimity. He strives to no goal.

18 THE SAGE is aware that his happiness, his peace
of mind, does not depend upon what others think of
him. He understands that those whose programming –
genes and conditioning – resonates with his own body-
mind organism may 'like' him, while others may not. He
is not really concerned with either.

19 IT IS SAID that awakening is always sudden,
but deliverance gradual. 'Deliverance' happens for the
unified mind, in accord with the Cosmic Law, when all
self-centered striving ceases, doubts and reconciliations
vanish, and life flows in all innocence. Nothing clings
to the sage, and the sage clings to nothing. In his world
of 'amness' and 'suchness', there is neither the Self nor
the other-than-Self to be concerned with the unreality of
life. The sage rests in perfect harmony with his mantra:
Only a happening, never a doer.

20 THE SAGE is certainly aware of his ego as a separate entity; however, because of the absence of a sense of personal doership, there is such a deep sense of withdrawal that when he hears anything said about him, his immediate reaction is: 'Who, me?!'

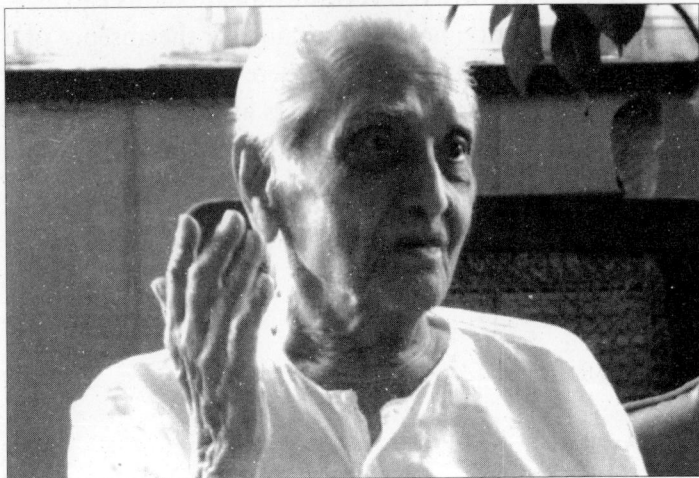

HAPPINESS IS...
Staying Connected With The Source

A talk with Ramesh

RAMESH   What brought you here?

AYEESHA   To India?

RAMESH   No, to me!

AYEESHA   ...Because I have a friend and she said she
really enjoyed listening to you.

RAMESH   So, are you interested in what we talk about?

AYEESHA   Of course!

RAMESH   She told you what I talk about?

AYEESHA   Yes. Little, I have very little brain. I have been here in India since six months. I understand very little. But I have a question. My experience is that when I am left without my sorrow, I am filled with this bubbling joy and it's wonderful...

RAMESH   Joy? Yes?

AYEESHA   Hmmm. I mean I am filled with happiness but I don't stay like this, living constantly connected to the Source. When I am connected to it – fantastic! And then I don't know what happens.

RAMESH   Now, wait a minute. When do you get disconnected from the Source?

AYEESHA   When I think of how awful a person I am! When I think of what I might have done wrong in my life. All this is like an obsession... I must bring this to some stage to look at it, I did this awful thing...

RAMESH   And when do you get over it?

AYEESHA   When?

RAMESH   When do you again get connected to the Source?

AYEESHA   When I have just left it to be. I feel like a guest saying, 'Please draw a chair and sit there.' And then the misery changes, that is my experience. And then I notice nature, I notice somebody's beautiful face and then I am back again. This is my experience. I would like not to go through it.

RAMESH Wouldn't you like to get rid of that all the time and be in connection with the Source all the time?

AYEESHA Yes, and that is my question... how?

RAMESH So, your question really is, 'Is it possible to stay connected to the Source all the time?'

AYEESHA Right, sure.

RAMESH That's the whole point! Is it possible to stay connected with the Source all the time? That's the real question? What do you say, Dominique [*to another visitor*], is it possible?

DOMINIQUE Yes.

RAMESH It is possible! It is possible to stay connected

to the Source all the time and therefore be happy. But first question is – Why do you get disconnected? When do you get disconnected from the Source? You get disconnected from the Source when you blame and condemn someone for doing something, either yourself or the other. When you blame and condemn yourself you hate yourself and when you blame and condemn the other, you hate the other and the moment you hate anybody you are disconnected from the Source, isn't that simple?

AYEESHA It is simple, but how do I stop that when I realize it is happening?

RAMESH So, the first question is: When do I get disconnected from the Source? When do I condemn anyone for anything – either myself or the other? When do I condemn anyone for anything? When he does something which I think he shouldn't do. Isn't that right?

AYEESHA   Yes, okay.

RAMESH   So there is only one way and that is not to condemn anybody. You can't imagine that, that there is only one way, a simple way...

AYEESHA   You mean to say, to love them or to love myself, is that what...?

RAMESH   Well, how do you love someone you don't like?! Therefore I am not talking of liking anybody or disliking anybody, make no mistake. Why? – that is the basic question. Let us say, suppose you are in a party of 20 to 30 people and nobody knows anybody. You also don't know anybody. Now in that group, if all 20 of them meet at the same time, what do you see happening after five minutes, ten minutes? What *does* happen? Again I am talking from personal experience, I am not parroting anybody's words and moreover I am talking from daily living, therefore what I say is of considerable value. What I say is what I feel from experience, not what somebody else says and secondly it concerns the daily living and not some imaginary perfect life.

AYEESHA So when you feel a condemning thought for someone, what do you do?

RAMESH Wait, let's go step by step.

AYEESHA Okay!

RAMESH So, where we were? Yes, I asked you to tell me from your personal experience that if 20-25-30 people decide to meet or happen to meet and no one knows the other then ten minutes after they have met, what is the absolutely natural happening? Do all thirty of them get together and become one healthy family, do they become one brotherhood – twenty people get together, do they become a healthy brotherhood?

AYEESHA   No, not usually.

RAMESH   Not likely! What do you find? Again, I am speaking from daily living – almost invariably what you will find is a group of 20-30 people gets spread into four or five different groups. Isn't that right?

AYEESHA   Yes.

RAMESH   What makes four or five people get together in a group? They don't know each other, nobody knows anyone – you could say each one joins someone whom they consider handsome! You could say if someone considers herself an ugly one, she would prefer to join someone uglier than herself. So, whatever the standard, my point is, 20-30 people automatically divide themselves into five or six groups. Is that not a fact? I repeat, I am talking from daily living. On what basis do 4-5 groups form by themselves?

DOMINIQUE   Well, according to their nature, they will be attracted or repulsed by the other.

RAMESH   Quite right, absolutely correct. Therefore, my point is, every body-mind organism has natural preferences for no reason at all, positive or negative. You like the fat person because may be you are fat but someone likes a thin person. Or even as simple as, someone likes the blue colour and the other likes the yellow colour. So preferences, positive or negative, are the natural functions of any body-mind organism and the natural preferences try to come together. The natural functions will almost smell it, almost feel it – 'I like that thing, it is my type.' Isn't that right? 'If I have to spend next 20 minutes chit chatting for nothing, I will go to him.' So, my point is within 5-10 minutes, 4 or 5 groups form by themselves.

So, for these five separate groups would you say that they are detached from the Source or disconnected from the Source? Five different groups automatically form themselves, are these five groups separated from the Source? When is there any separation from the Source? There is separation from the Source – when one person from one group sees another person do something and he says I don't like what he has done, in this society it is not done, it is not to be done, it should not have been done – then you have condemned him. Once you have condemned anybody for anything, your connection with the Source is broken because the other is as much connected to the Source as you are!

Incidentally, what I am talking about now is, believe me, true spirituality, true Advaita. So, what I was saying is, when someone condemns somebody for doing something which is not acceptable to him (the first person), his connection with the Source is broken. So, what is the one way you do not get disconnected from the Source, never get disconnected from the Source and be happy through out the day, whether you are in pleasure or in pain? What is the ultimate happiness every human being wants? To be happy all the time!

What is happiness? For me, happiness is: never to be disconnected from the Source throughout the day, whether in pleasure or in pain. Whereas, if someone says that for me it is simple to be happy, I want to be in pleasure all the time, the fact is, that can never be! Because the very basis of life is duality; sometimes pleasure, sometimes pain. Nobody knows whether the next moment will bring pleasure or pain. Nobody knows the total amount of pleasure and pain one has to accept in one's life, that all is already predetermined. The movie of life has already been done, it is done for millions of years and is in the can and we are witnessing the movie frame by frame. Whatever has happened at any time has already been filmed and framed.

My connection with the Source, once it is broken, gets connected again when that which has broken the connection, stops, the connection is then again reconnected.

So, the important thing is, for me to be continuously happy, my connection with the Source is never broken. It is not that once the connection is broken, it is broken for all the time. It can't. That connection is for the whole life. Therefore what is unhappiness? Unhappiness is my connection with the Source being broken very often. More often my connection with the Source is broken, the more unhappy I am. See, what I mean? Therefore the fewer times my connection with the Source is broken, the less unhappy I am. If my connection with the Source is never broken, I am never unhappy.

Isn't that beautiful and simple?! Simple formula for being happy in life – the basis of which is not to hate anyone at any time for doing anything, myself or the other. If I blame myself, I hate myself. If I blame some one else I hate someone else. The moment I condemn someone, my connection is broken and that is what happens with most of the people. How do you find most people? Always grumbling about someone or the other – 'He said this to me, he said that to me'; 'He did this to me, he did that to someone else.' Isn't that right?

And what is the only way, the only way, not to break the connection with the Source? There is only one way, and that is, I need not ever condemn anyone for anything and thereby not to have my connection with the Source ever broken. Therefore a very simple formula for not getting the connection with the Source ever broken is not to condemn anyone for anything! Simple formula, isn't it?

AYEESHA Simple formula... [*Thinking over*]

RAMESH Let us understand this. You condemn yourself for doing something which hurts someone, which hurts you or which hurts someone you love. Whom do you condemn? When and whom do you condemn, at any time, yourself or the other? Again and again I repeat, I don't talk of high philosophy, I leave it to those who have plenty of time to waste and plenty of energy to waste but for a busy person like me, my focal question is, 'For someone like us, who by the grace of God is reasonably comfortable in life – for which we have to be eternally grateful to God – and who also has the common sense to know that the very basis of life is uncertainty, no one can know whether the next moment will bring pleasure or pain. No one can know how long one is going to live. No one can know how much pleasure or how much pain one is going to experience in life, the entire basis of life being uncertainty.

Now, first and foremost, let me be clear that I am not interested in making life easier for others. I consider God who has created this world to be powerful enough to look after his own world. I do not consider it my responsibility to better the condition of this world.

Therefore I am only concerned with my selfish motive

of being happy in my daily life. In my daily living, I am concerned with being happy, in *this* life. And in what conditions? I have told you the conditions are clear enough – by the grace of God, we are reasonably comfortable in life for which we are grateful to God. We have to accept that life means uncertainty. You never know whether the next moment is going to bring pleasure or pain. You don't know how much pleasure or pain you are going to have in your whole life. So, in these uncertain times, not knowing what the next moment will bring, what do I consider happiness, which I want in this life?

That is what I am concerned with, that is what I talk about and that for me is the religion and that is why I have written a simple book *A Personal Religion Of Your Own*. I have thrown all the religions out of the window. What is the use of religion which makes people fight among themselves since thousand of years, killing each other? Therefore I said I want a religion of my own, so I have got a personal religion of my own and I talk about 'a personal religion of my own' which keeps me connected with the Source all the time and thus keeps me happy through the daily life.

AYEESHA In your personal religion, if you find a condemning thought, what will you do?

RAMESH   I am sorry?

AYEESHA If you had a condemning thought, then as soon as you notice that, 'Oh! I am judging this person," how...?

RAMESH   In my personal religion, I do not have a condemning thought for anybody.

AYEESHA But if I do have?

RAMESH Then you have not followed my personal religion. Therefore, I keep repeating, because it needs repeating – The whole point is, in order to be happy I do not want my connection with the Source ever broken. My definition of unhappiness is, my connection with the Source being broken. I repeat, I consider my happiness to be that in which my connection with the Source is not broken. If my connection to the Source is broken – it is unhappiness.

We talk of happiness and unhappiness – what is happiness and what is unhappiness? Happiness is more confused with the word pleasure *and my happiness has nothing to do with pleasure.* Pleasure concerns some item which gives me pleasure for sometime, but my happiness depends on nothing but myself! My happiness depends on my attitude to life and not on the pleasures which life brings – the most important difference.

Therefore, according to me, whether I am in pleasure in the moment or in pain in the moment, it is never in my control and what is not in my control, why should I bother about it? I am only concerned with that which is in my control and what is in my control is – whether to keep my connection with the Source totally unbroken or not. So the most important thing is – when is my connection with the Source broken? The moment I condemn anyone for anything, the connection with the Source is broken and I am unhappy till my connection is again made.

Is it possible to live in such a way in daily life without the connection with the Source ever being broken? In deep sleep, there is no such question. This question arises only in the waking state. Therefore, in the waking state, when

I am living my daily life, is it possible *not* to break my connection with the Source at all? The answer is – *'Yes!'* And that is, during my daily life, whatever is anybody doing, I do not condemn anybody.

The question arises – if a miser refuses to pay a single pie to a suffering beggar, should I not condemn him, do I not naturally condemn him? How can I not condemn him? What is the answer? The answer is: I do not condemn a miser for being a miser. *A miser did not choose to be a miser* just as a generous man did not choose to be a generous man. Being miser or generous is part of his genes over which no human being has any control. A saint did not choose to be a saint, a psychopath did not choose to be a psychopath. There is a generous man or a good man or a bad man or a psychopath… it is what is generally known as the very nature of the person concerned over which no human being has had any control. It was based entirely on the genes and conditioning of the person concerned.

If I am able to accept totally that no one actually does anything, that the human being is merely a three dimensional object through which the Source or God or Pure Energy or Consciousness functions and brings about whatever is supposed to happen according to God's Will or Cosmic Law. If I am able to accept totally – the human being, a three dimensional object, cannot do anything except witness whatever is happening, a happening which had to happen at that time at that moment, the way it happened, according to God's Will/Cosmic Law – 'Thy will be done' – then I do not condemn. Whatever happens at any moment is a happening according to God's Will/ Cosmic Law. No one can help any one, no one can harm anyone. We can only witness whatever is happening as a natural outcome of the genes in the human body organism or the work produced by the primal energy through that instrument according to whatever is considered necessary according to God's Will and the individual person's destiny.

Everything in the world is a happening which happens according to God's Will and whether it helps someone or hurts someone is according to the destiny of the person concerned. No individual entity has any power to hurt anyone or help anyone. It's only a three dimensional object. Therefore if I am able to accept totally that human being is incapable of doing anything; that every thing in the world is a happening according to God's Will/Cosmic Law; that everything happens through the body-mind organism spontaneously according to the genes; that no individual is capable of doing anything good or bad, then how can I condemn anybody for anything?

Now, why do I condemn myself – I condemn myself because I feel I should have done that and instead of that I did this. But did I do it? It happened because it had to happen according to God's Will/Cosmic Law. Then the question arises – does it mean that I can do whatever bad thing that I like and say 'I am not the doer'? I will say, 'Yes' – according to your heart, according to your conscience, according to God.

But in your daily life, the society in which you are living, considers every action as your action. You may agree and God may agree, that it is not your action but the society considers it as *your* action and society will punish you or reward you according to existing social regulations and legal provisions which you have to accept as your destiny but as far as you are concerned, as far as God is concerned, you cannot commit a sin. When you are not capable of doing anything, how can you do a meritorious act or commit a sin? But as far as the society is concerned, society will judge according to the social regulations and legal provisions and reward you or punish you.

What I have described to you is daily living. So, this is 'my personal religion'. It is the simplest of religions to follow and whether you are able to follow it or not, is your destiny. Do you follow what I mean?

So, any questions?!

DOMINIQUE Well, I will point...

RAMESH Wait a minute. You have understood this, haven't you?

DOMINIQUE Yes.

RAMESH   So, is it possible to live my personal religion in life? In other words, how has this teaching affected your personal daily living to the extent that it has?

DOMINIQUE   Well, I would say that just on percentage basis, I could say that where there was a large percentage of unhappiness due to disconnection from the Source, there is now a small percentage of unhappiness. Now, the condemning has come right down.

RAMESH   Would you say that until you have the total acceptance, that until the total acceptance happens, some involvement does happen and moreover you get punished too, as the doer of your actions... and that is accepted?

DOMINIQUE   Yes.

RAMESH   So, until that happens, and while this is

happening and before this understanding took place; in your own estimate, what would you say in your daily life was the percentage of happiness and the percentage of unhappiness. Straight question! Well, it's a guess but I would only say that you have to be honest.

DOMINIQUE I would say before I came to you, I was about 75% unhappy.

RAMESH   Only 75%?

DOMINIQUE Yes.

RAMESH   I would be inclined to say it was 90%. Anyway, 75% unhappiness and 25% happiness. I would like to say your previous percentage was 90% unhappiness and 10% happiness. Anyway, what would your percentage be now?

DOMINIQUE   On this score, I would say about 10% of the time, disconnection from the Source arises.

RAMESH   So, in other words, you will say it is 90% happiness, now?

DOMINIQUE   90% of the time I see what happens as a happening and 10% of the time I get involved in it.

RAMESH   I agree! And in 90% happiness, only 10% unhappiness that remains, is overshadowed.

DOMINIQUE   Yes.

RAMESH   The 10% unhappiness that remains is almost overshadowed by the 90% happiness. So overall you don't care a damn now, whether there is 10% unhappiness?

DOMINIQUE Right, yes.

RAMESH In other words, life now presents no problem. You are a happy man.

DOMINIQUE Yes! I would say that there seems to be certain burden sitting there but whether that burden is there or not, I don't care so much.

RAMESH That is the point ! The 10% burden... who cares?!

DOMINIQUE If God's Will is there or not there, it has to happen anyway. So, why am I going to try and rid of it?

RAMESH In other words, now, what you are saying is that the 10% burden I wouldn't even bother to remove.

Dominique   Right! There is a preference to be without it
but if it is there, it is there.

Ramesh   I wouldn't even bother to remove it! Let it get
dissolved! I entirely agree Dominique, I entirely agree. So
for Dominique, an average person, I mean he never has
been a saintly person, has he been?

Dominique   No.

Ramesh   Therefore, my point is, even for an average
person, my 'personal religion of my own' helps to be
happy. What is happiness? Happiness means being
connected with the Source all the time. And what is
enlightenment? What would you say is enlightenment?
[*Asking Dominique*] Would you not say being connected
with the Source 90%? Therefore, now the latest book
that is coming on Guru Pournima day, 18th of this month

– I have got a hundred hardbound copies, I value it so much, to be given away to those who come on Guru Pournima day – and the title of the book is *Pursue 'Happiness' And Get Enlightened*. It will rub the edges of almost any of the spiritual masters.

All the religious men say – it is not an easy thing, you have to work hard for it, meditate two hours a day, go and visit the temple, do this, do that, don't do this, don't do that and then you may get enlightened. And more importantly, nobody, and I mean nobody, will give you an answer to the question: 'I am supposed to pursue enlightenment but why should I pursue enlightenment? Tell me, why should I pursue enlightenment?' But nobody will give you an answer to that. Secondly, 'What will enlightenment do for me for the rest of my life that I didn't have before?'

If I want to get something, I am supposed to get something. For example, I want to get food, what will the food do for me? It will satisfy my hunger! Similarly, I want to get enlightenment, what will enlightenment give me for the rest of my life that I didn't have before? What do I want enlightenment for? Nobody would give me the answers to these questions, which were the two most important answers I wanted.

That's why I keep saying I pursued enlightenment for 40 years and ended up in frustration. Then after I retired from work, for the remaining few years of my life I decided – I will throw enlightenment out of the window and I will seek personal happiness. I shall pursue the purely selfish objective of personal happiness and I did and I got enlightened too. The most important question which I had to go into, in that pursuit, was, what do I mean by happiness? I had decided to pursue happiness. The most important thing I had to decide was, what do I mean by happiness? Obviously, I am reasonably comfortable in life, I have enjoyed pleasures, I know what pleasure is! I have not enjoyed all the pleasures in life but even if I did enjoy all the pleasures in life, would I still not be seeking? What is this happiness I am seeking which has nothing to do with the pleasures in life? And the most important conclusion I came to, before I even started, was that the happiness I am seeking has nothing to do with the flow of life but my attitude to life.

Next important question: attitude to life is too vast a thing; specifically what do I mean by attitude to life? And I came to the conclusion that attitude to life can only mean attitude towards the other, whoever the other is, my closest relative, my neighbour, someone connected with my business or occupation or someone not connected with anything at all i.e. a total stranger.

Whoever the other is, what is my relationship, in fact, what has been my relationship so far which has not brought me the happiness but unhappiness?

The most important and the honest answer I could get was – my attitude towards the other, whoever the other, whether it is my brother or a stranger, was one of suspicion and fear, fear that he may take something away from me, fear that he may come between my getting something.

In other words, the basis of my attitude towards the other, whoever the other, has been, one of suspicion, fear and rivalry and therefore I am unhappy and therefore I am seeking happiness. Therefore, for me to be happy, I have to have a totally harmonious relationship with the other. And the only way I can have a totally harmonious relationship with the other is to accept totally that he cannot harm me even if he wants to. He may want to hurt me but unless it is also God's Will to hurt me, he can't hurt me, I can't hurt him either. Both of us are only three dimensional objects, incapable of doing anything, through which only God or the Primal Energy or Consciousness is functioning and bringing about whatever is supposed to happen according to God's Will/Cosmic Law. We can only witness whatever is happening. And whether that happening is supposed to hurt me or help me is again according to God's Will/Cosmic Law. Through which person or body-mind organism, the happening happens is again according to God's Will/Cosmic Law, although the society considers each action as my action, your action, his action or her action and appropriately deals with it.

So, this is the total '*Personal Religion Of Your Own*'. It is an extremely inexpensive book. Therefore, I say, not only read it, enjoy it and be happy but also present as many copies as you can to your friends and make them happy. Even more important, give as many copies as you can to your enemies and may be turn them into your friends.

Any questions?

VIMAL   I have one question. Just now you said that you have to accept everything as God's Will. I find it difficult to accept the gang rape of a young girl as the Cosmic Law or God's Will. I mean, rape or murder or even small children being abused. I find that very disturbing and that is the time when disconnection takes place.

RAMESH   I see. And who finds it very difficult, a three dimensional object? Whatever you have seen, does it make a stone feel bad? Does it make a stone on which the gang rape took place, feel bad? No! That is one aspect of it and second aspect of it is, everything that happens in this world, the basis of it is duality. The Source or God is the only singularity. God is the only singularity; 'Shiva', 'Brahman', whatever you call it, That one Source has become the manifested duality. And duality in manifestation means the existence of everything in both its interconnected opposites; the wildest deed and the most beautiful deed, the saint and the psychopath!

VIMAL I find it difficult to accept that. I find it difficult.

RAMESH For whom?

VIMAL For me, for me.

RAMESH For a three dimensional object! The only thing you must never ever forget is, that however great you are a person or however bad you are a person, you are fundamentally a three dimensional object incapable of feeling anything.

VIMAL But I am still not a stone on which it happens. I am a person with...

RAMESH Aah, yes, therefore what does Vimal have to do?

VIMAL Well, I can't do anything, I feel so helpless.

RAMESH Therefore, what does Vimal have to do? What she has been doing all her life! Enjoy the pleasure and suffer the pain. If it is pleasure, you enjoy the pleasure, this is a pain and you have to suffer the pain about which nobody can do anything. You are complaining, I am having pain for twenty years, I find it difficult to bear, but it's your destiny. If it were twenty years of pleasure, would you have complained?

VIMAL Well, nobody complains about pleasure.

RAMESH Ah, that is the point! Nobody complains
about pleasure. Everybody complains about pain
and this is one of the kinds of pain which you have
to accept as your destiny and yet, make no mistake,
*in any situation, it is your birthright to do anything
you want to do.* It is your birthright and therefore
when Vimal sees a woman being gang-raped, it is her
birthright to do anything. If she happens to have a
walking stick with her, it is her birthright to hit them
on the head till they fall down dead. Hit them on
heads, break their bones, break their necks, break their
legs, break their noses. Beat them right and left and
take the help of surrounding people also, if possible.
Do whatever you like, that is your birthright but at the

same time, the results of your birthright, you have to accept, from the society. Okay?

VIMAL   Thank you.

RAMESH   Yes, Ma'm, your name is... [*Turning to another visitor who wants to ask something*]

VISITOR   My name is Priya. That is my dad [*pointing to her father, sitting there*]

PRIYA   Does meditation have any role in helping you reconnect back to the Source?

RAMESH   Yes, yes, it does! Yes, it does! Meditation helps you to heal the crack which has happened and which has disconnected you from the Source. Something has happened which has disconnected you. Your mind is

restless and therefore you meditate. And meditation in
that time, meditation in that time when your mind is
free of concepts, that is the time when you reconnect
with the Source. Okay? Now, your next question.

PRIYA   You keep talking about duality and singularity.
What is duality? What does it mean?

RAMESH   God means Singularity. 'One'. Basis of
manifestation is duality, beginning with male and
female. Without male and female, duality cannot
persist. Beginning with male and female, beautiful and
ugly, true and false, greater and lesser, birth and death,
pleasure and pain, everything is interconnected. That's
what is meant by duality... How old are you?

PRIYA   I am thirty-one.

RAMESH Are you married?

PRIYA No.

RAMESH What do you do in life to earn a living?

PRIYA I work for an investment bank in New York. I had first come here in 1997-98. The first time I came here, I didn't understand much and slowly I have really developed an interest in the subject. I am really fascinated after I read *I Am That* by Nisargadatta Maharaj and I have been interested.

RAMESH So, both in practical life and this together, very lucky, very good.

PRIYA I like certain things which are not considered very great by Hindu standards, like I like to earn money, I like to live a good lifestyle, I like going out with friends. I like all those things but I am still...

RAMESH   Why do you think you shouldn't?

PRIYA   My grandparents tell me drinking is not good. I am not an alcoholic, but I like doing – I mean I like eating out or drinking.

RAMESH   You are not an alcoholic?

PRIYA   No.

RAMESH   But you like an occasional drink.

PRIYA   Yes.

RAMESH   What the hell is wrong with it?

PRIYA I don't think so.

RAMESH One thing I can tell you – you have an occasional drink, your connection with the Source is not broken. [*Loud laughter from the audience*]. Even with an occasional feast, your connection with Source is not broken. Okay?

PRIYA Okay. Thank you.

RAMESH You say that the purpose of Advaita is to be happy. Why? Because our very nature is happiness! If our very nature was stomach ache, we would not try to get rid of stomach ache. Since our very nature is happiness, that is why the desire arises for something or the other, a desire arises and we feel that when the desire will be satisfied, we will be happy. However, though we feel that when the desire will be satisfied it will make us happy but one has to be very careful now and understand very clearly as to what is happiness! One has to understand what is happiness and what is not happiness!

Therefore, Advaita is our nature which is happiness, so happiness is our very nature. I repeat, Advaita, our nature, our very nature is happiness. Okay?

PRIYA Yes, thank you.

PRIYA'S FATHER Can I ask you something? Rather can I say something? I have been exposed to this teaching for quite a while and I have really enjoyed the whole journey.

RAMESH What are you in life?

PRIYA'S FATHER I retired recently. I was a marine engineer.

RAMESH   Okay. So, what is your problem?

PRIYA'S FATHER   Right now, when you are explaining, I
am gathering that basically happiness is not judging, not
criticizing, that is what happiness is. Because judging or
criticizing takes you away from your true nature, because
everybody is connected to that 'One' and the moment you
criticize someone else...

RAMESH   Your connection with the Source is broken!

PRIYA'S FATHER   Yes, but this is just one side of the coin, the
other side being 'no one does anything'. If you can accept
that then only you can accept this, isn't it? Two sides of
the same coin?

RAMESH   Why do you think somebody is wrong because
what you think is right? Why do you condemn at all? Why

condemn at all?

PRIYA'S FATHER   It suits me, it suits my morality.

RAMESH   Therefore, you have not accepted the basic duality of life. Basic duality of life is – if there is one, there is the other.

PRIYA'S FATHER   So, only if you accept that no one does anything then the whole riddle gets solved.

RAMESH   And the basis of manifestation is duality – where there is beautiful, there is ugly; where there is saint, there is psychopath; where there is illness, there is health.

PRIYA'S FATHER   True.

RAMESH   Okay? [*Turning to another visitor*] Yes...?

ROHIT   Many, many insights have occurred sitting here and I would like to comment on one of the insights that I have got because of the narration of incident of gang rape. You say, love and hate are interconnected opposites, society judges and condemns the rapist and compensates the object of rape. They are interconnected opposites.

RAMESH   Yes, and that is the basis of law.

ROHIT   Will not the compassion arise for the rapist as well, with the understanding that the rapist was compelled by his destiny to commit the rape? I just want to clarify that the attitude of the sage will always be that of compassion, is it not so?

RAMESH   The attitude of the sage? No. The sage has no

attitude. The biological reaction, the biological attitude
of the sage will be that of compassion, just as the
biological reaction in some other person would be rage.
Two people see the same thing. In one case there will
be rage, in another person there may be compassion.
Both are biological reactions, according to the genes and
conditioning. No individual reaction.

ROHIT That arising of compassion would not be even
inconsistent with stopping of the rape, through the sage?

RAMESH Arising of the compassion; you are free to
do whatever you like. Therefore, arising of the rage,
you may want to hit the other fellow. Arising of the
compassion, also, you may want to hit the fellow.

VIMAL So, it is easy for me to accept the duality if I am
not the victim. But if I am a victim, how do I explain to

myself that this is in duality? What I am saying is, from the victim's point of view it is not easy to explain.

RAMESH From the victim's point of view, it is not easy to explain the pain. Someone suffering from cancer for last five years, from the victim's point of view, what kind of explanation can you give? Is there any explanation?

VIMAL No.

RAMESH That is the point; except that the pain is to be borne. That's all. It is a pain and the pain has to be borne. Pain and pleasure – pleasure, you enjoy the pleasure; pain, you bear the pain. It is one's destiny.

The body is a robot.
You are Consciousness as ego. Consciousness, functioning through and within your body, identifies with your body and the name given to it. This identified Consciousness: you, the ego, experiences life as it happens automatically, according to cosmic functioning, also called God's will.
You, Consciousness as ego, experience even the deepest spiritual experience only by God's will, or the movement of primal energy or Consciousness, which is all there is.